DNA Is Here to Stay

by Dr. Fran Balkwill
illustrated by Mic Rolph

Carolrhoda Books, Inc./Minneapolis

This edition first published 1993 by Carolrhoda Books, Inc.

Text copyright © 1992 by Fran Balkwill
Illustrations copyright © 1992 by Mic Rolph

First published 1992 by HarperCollins Publishers Ltd, London, England.
All rights to this edition reserved by Carolrhoda Books, Inc.

Library of Congress Cataloging-in-Publication Data

Balkwill, Francis R.
    DNA is here to stay / by Fran Balkwill ; illustrated by Mic Rolph.
        p.   cm.
    Summary: A simple explanation of what DNA is and what it does in
the body.
    ISBN 0-87614-763-5
    1. DNA – Juvenile literature. [1. DNA.] I. Rolph, Mic, ill.
II. Title.
QP624.B35   1993
574.87′3282 – dc20   92-4802
                                                                CIP
                                                                 AC

Manufactured in the United States of America

1 2 3 4 5 6 7 8 9 10 02 01 00 99 98 97 96 95 94 93

Once there was a tiny cell, smaller than a grain of sand. Although that cell was very small, it carried an incredibly complicated and amazingly clever plan.

A plan to make a unique living creature...

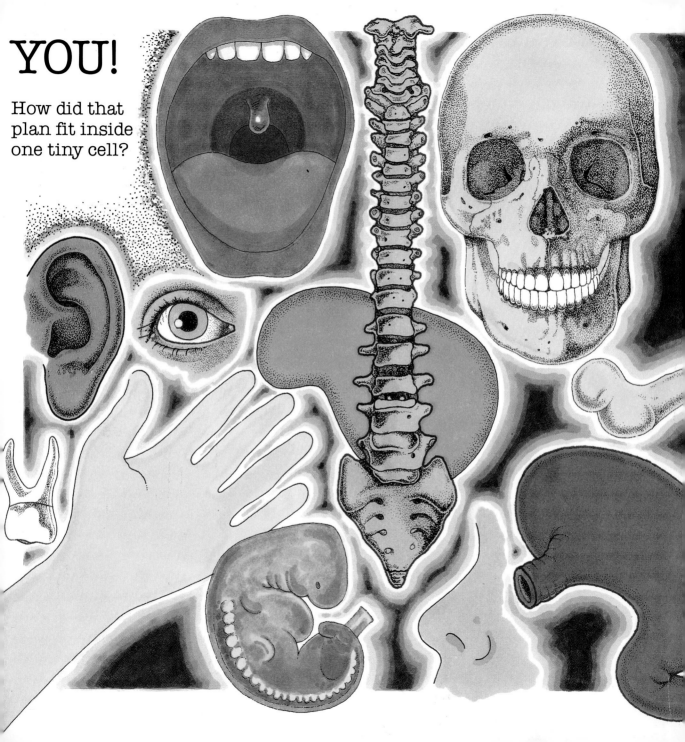

YOU!

How did that plan fit inside one tiny cell?

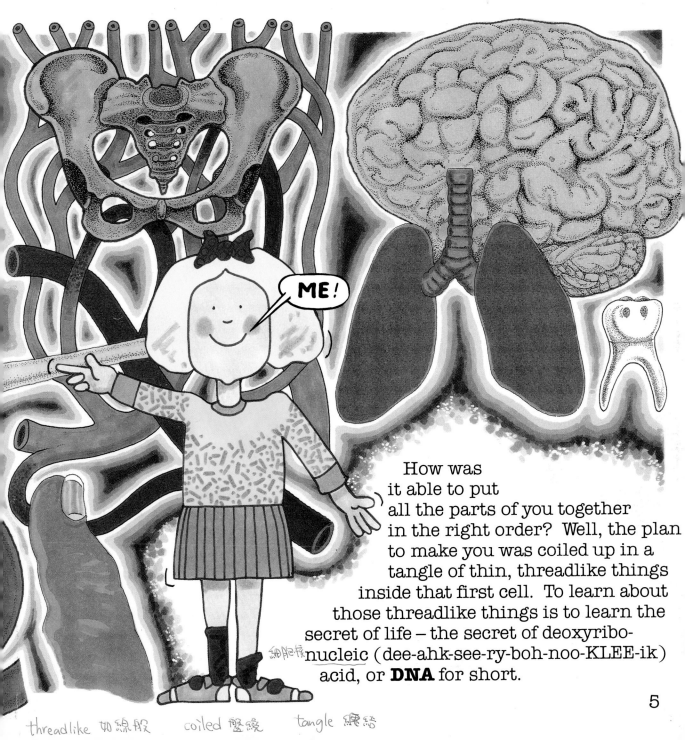

ME!

How was
it able to put
all the parts of you together
in the right order? Well, the plan
to make you was coiled up in a
tangle of thin, threadlike things
inside that first cell. To learn about
those threadlike things is to learn the
secret of life — the secret of deoxyribo-
nucleic (dee-ahk-see-ry-boh-noo-KLEE-ik)
acid, or **DNA** for short.

5

threadlike 叩線般   coiled 盤繞   tangle 纏結

Through a powerful electron microscope, the first cell that you started from would look something like this. So where's the DNA?

The DNA is coiled up in the center of the cell in 46 threadlike things called **chromosomes** (KRO-muh-sohmz). The threads are so thin that you can't even see them through the electron microscope.

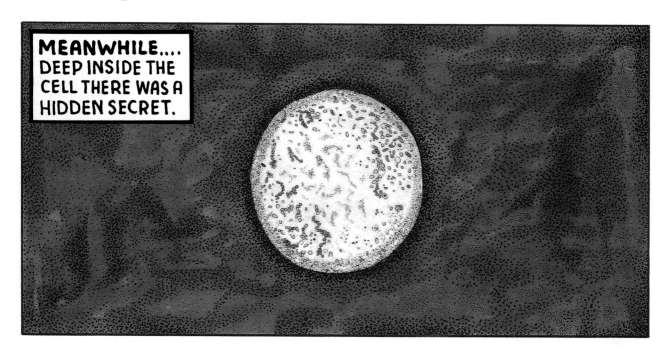

MEANWHILE.... DEEP INSIDE THE CELL THERE WAS A HIDDEN SECRET.

But if you unwound all the DNA from this single cell, it would stretch for about six feet (1¾ meters). And just as hard to imagine is the width of the DNA strands. You could fit about five million through the eye of a needle!

Look closely at the cell now. It is about to divide into two cells.
See the dark shapes in the center of the cell? Those are the
chromosomes. They are full of DNA.

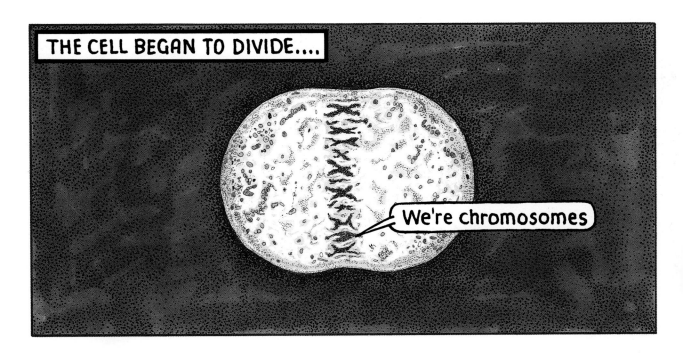

DNA coils up tightly when a cell is about to divide. That's why
you can see the chromosomes. They are shaped sort of like Xs.
All the information needed to make a unique human being is
contained within these chromosomes.

95 trillion Cells > 46 chromosomes >

What exactly does DNA look like? We'll unravel the DNA thread from one of the chromosomes. Pretend you've put on some magic glasses that can magnify everything 50 million times. (That would make a grain of sand look as big as a mountain!) Now you can easily see a thread of DNA and discover its most important secret.

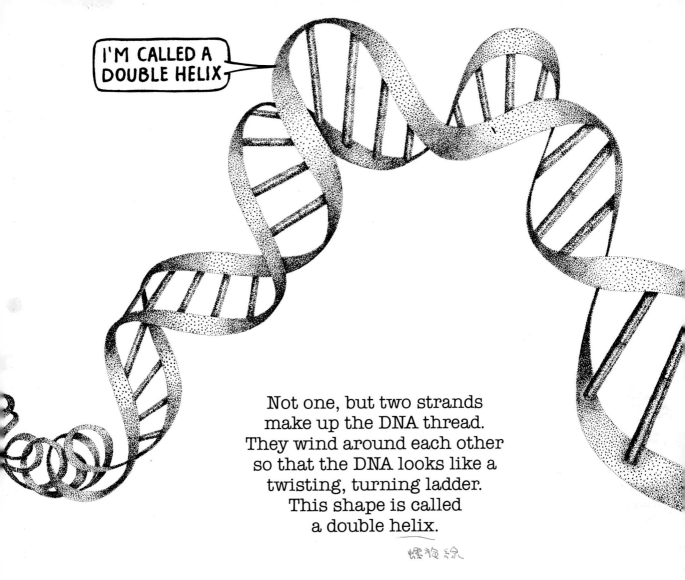

Not one, but two strands
make up the DNA thread.
They wind around each other
so that the DNA looks like a
twisting, turning ladder.
This shape is called
a double helix.

螺旋線

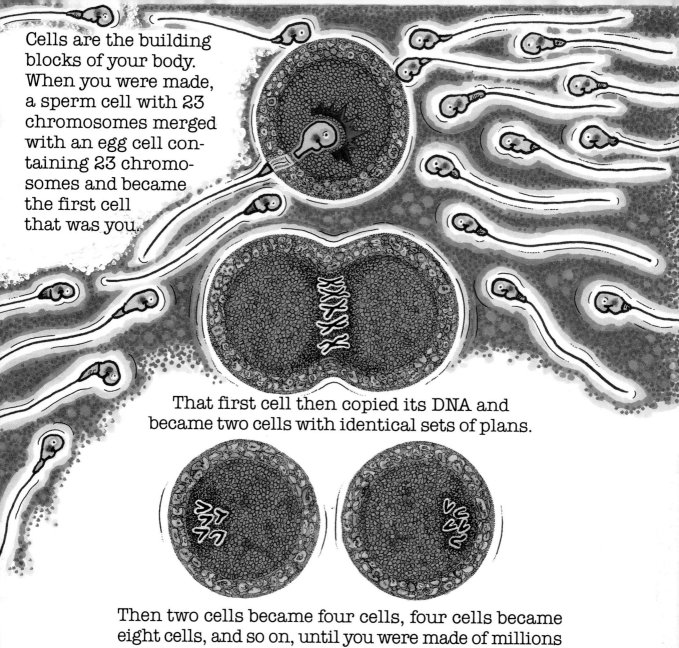

Cells are the building blocks of your body. When you were made, a sperm cell with 23 chromosomes merged with an egg cell containing 23 chromosomes and became the first cell that was you.

That first cell then copied its DNA and became two cells with identical sets of plans.

Then two cells became four cells, four cells became eight cells, and so on, until you were made of millions of cells. And the amazing thing is that each time one of those cells divided, its DNA plan was copied.

So each of your cells has the same DNA plan, and each of your cells has 46 chromosomes.

How exactly does DNA copy itself when cells divide?

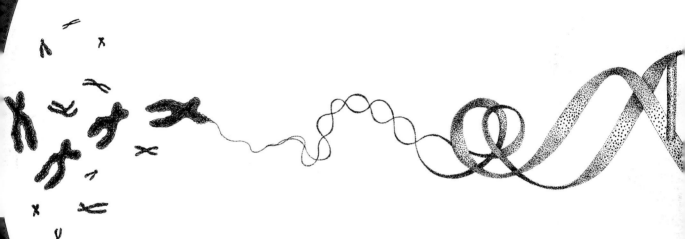

We'll unravel this DNA strand and find out.

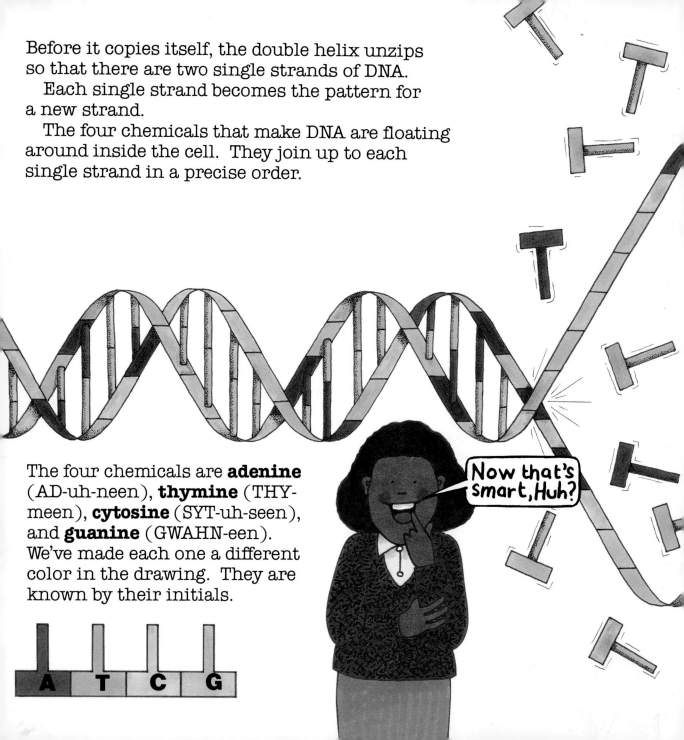

Before it copies itself, the double helix unzips so that there are two single strands of DNA.

Each single strand becomes the pattern for a new strand.

The four chemicals that make DNA are floating around inside the cell. They join up to each single strand in a precise order.

The four chemicals are **adenine** (AD-uh-neen), **thymine** (THY-meen), **cytosine** (SYT-uh-seen), and **guanine** (GWAHN-een). We've made each one a different color in the drawing. They are known by their initials.

A T C G

Now that's smart, Huh?

Can you see the order in which the chemicals are joined up?

Look very carefully at the DNA that is being copied in this picture.

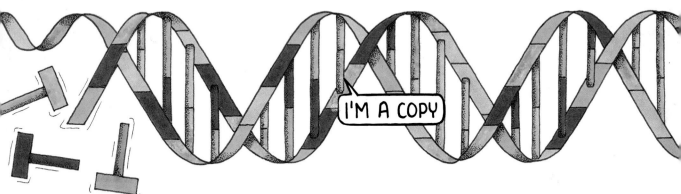

Chemical **A** always joins up with chemical **T**.
Chemical **T** always joins up with chemical **A**.
Chemical **C** always joins up with chemical **G**.
Chemical **G** always joins up with chemical **C**.

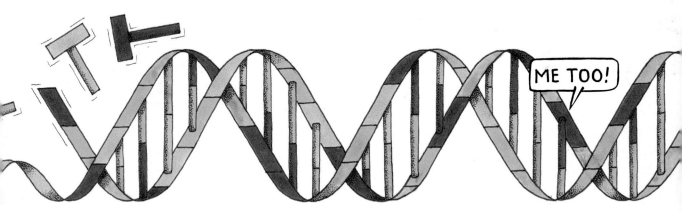

When the copying is finished, there are two identical DNA threads in each of the 46 chromosomes – one thread for each of the new cells. Now the cells divide.

Your DNA plan is like a secret code – a code so complicated that scientists only started to understand it as recently as the 1940s.

But how does this mysterious, twisting thread actually make you?

Well, it works like this.

Your body is made of cells.

Your cells are made of water, DNA, sugars, fats, and proteins. DNA is a code for making proteins.

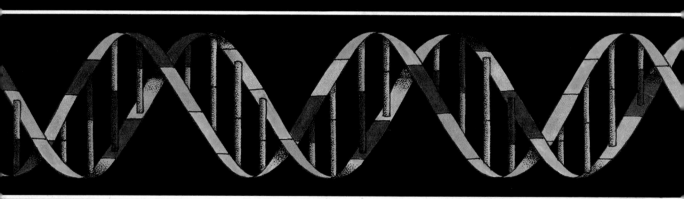

Proteins are important because they help a cell make other chemicals that it needs to do its job. Proteins make cells the shape and the color they are. Your DNA plan contains recipes for making about fifty thousand different types of proteins. The recipe for each protein is laid out in order along the DNA threads, using the chemicals **A, T, C,** and **G.** Each of these recipes is called a **gene** (JEEN).

So all you have to remember is that
DNA makes proteins, proteins make cells, and cells make YOU!

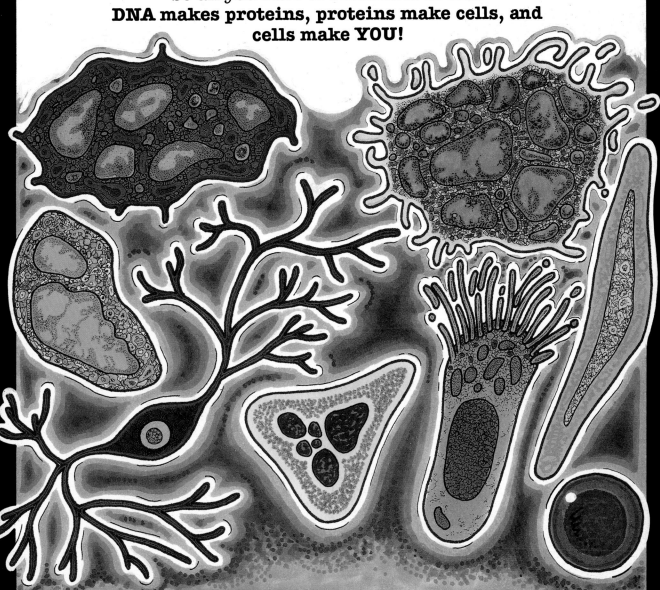

Turn the page to learn about some of your proteins.

Inside your blood cells, there is a protein called hemoglobin (HEE-muh-gloh-bin) that carries oxygen around your body.

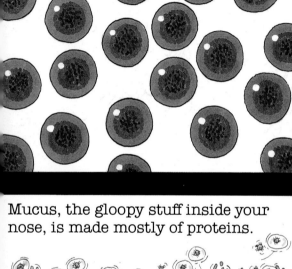

Cells in skin make a protein called melanin (MEL-uh-nin) that gives your skin its color and protects it from harmful rays in sunshine.

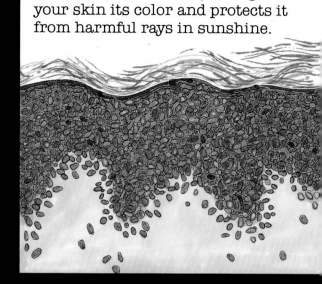

Mucus, the gloopy stuff inside your nose, is made mostly of proteins.

Waft!

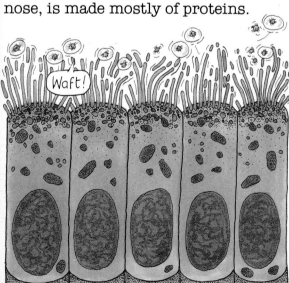

Your defender cells make proteins called antibodies that zap invader germs like viruses and bacteria.

Stomach cells make proteins called enzymes that help turn the food you eat into substances that give you energy.

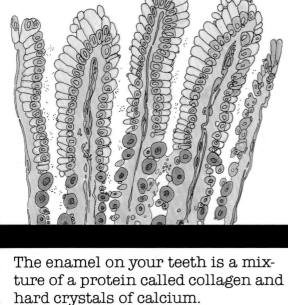

Cells on your head and body make hair. Hair is made of a protein called keratin.

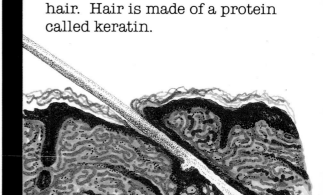

The enamel on your teeth is a mixture of a protein called collagen and hard crystals of calcium.

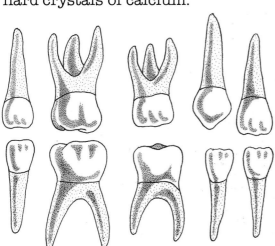

Actin and myosin are proteins that help your muscles expand and contract.

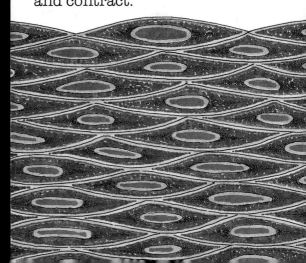

How does DNA act as a code for making these proteins?

To make it easier for you to see, we've straightened out part of the double helix. It's a little complicated, so take a deep breath, concentrate, and remember this strand is magnified about 50 million times. First a small part of the DNA unzips (we'll show you exactly how this happens on page 20). Now the recipe for a particular protein must be copied from one strand onto another strand.

Deep breath

This is the copy strand

I'm **U**!!

I've Unzipped!

The copy strand, called **RNA,** looks like a small piece of DNA – with one important difference. One chemical is different. The copy strand does not use any thymine (**T**). Instead it uses a chemical called **uracil** (YUR-uh-sil), or **U** for short.

As usual, if the DNA strand has a **T,** it copies **A,**
if the DNA strand has a **C,** it copies **G,** and
if the DNA strand has a **G,** it copies **C,**
but if the DNA strand has an A, it copies U.
Nobody knows exactly why this happens.

We'll use a tiny piece of one strand of the
DNA code for the protein hemoglobin to
show you exactly what happens.

The cell makes an RNA copy strand like this.

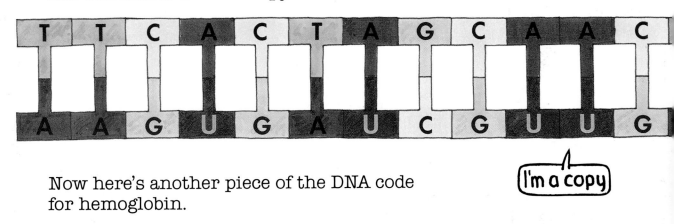

Now here's another piece of the DNA code
for hemoglobin.

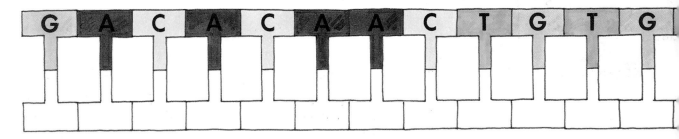

Can you figure out what the copy strand will be?

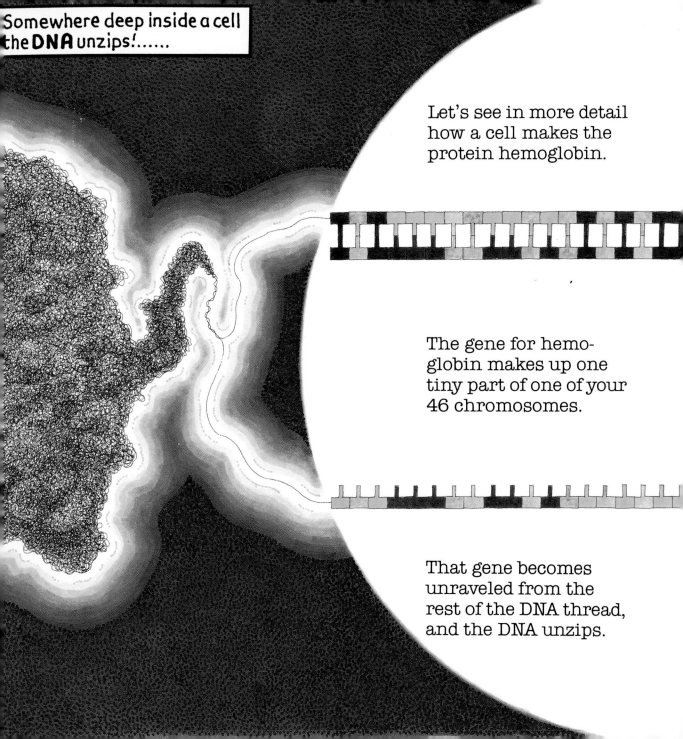

Somewhere deep inside a cell the **DNA** unzips!......

Let's see in more detail how a cell makes the protein hemoglobin.

The gene for hemoglobin makes up one tiny part of one of your 46 chromosomes.

That gene becomes unraveled from the rest of the DNA thread, and the DNA unzips.

It takes a cell about a minute to make a complete copy of the 1350 **A**s, **T**s, **C**s, and **G**s in the gene for hemoglobin.

If we were to write out the complete DNA recipe for hemoglobin at the size it is shown here, we would need another 36 pages, or about 200 feet (61 meters) of paper.

When the copy
strand is ready,
it travels to another
area of the cell to find
a **ribosome** (RY-buh-sohm).
The ribosome is like a micro-
scopic workbench that holds
the copy strand fast.

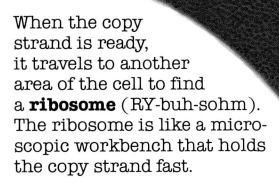

All proteins are made from
chemicals called **amino
acids.** The thousands of different
proteins in your body are made from
20 amino acids joined up together in
every possible combination. Our copy
strand has instructions for the
particular combination of amino
acids that make hemoglobin.

The ribosome reads the instructions on the copy strand. As it
moves along the copy strand,
it joins amino acids together
like beads of a necklace.

The copy strand is now complete and leaves the chromosome.

The copy strand sticks to the ribosome, which reads the **A**s, **C**s, **G**s, and **U**s. Now the ribosome knows the order in which to join up the amino acids.

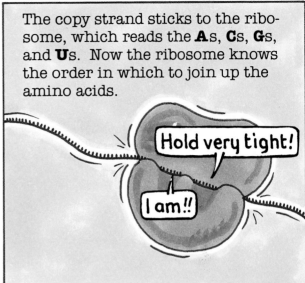

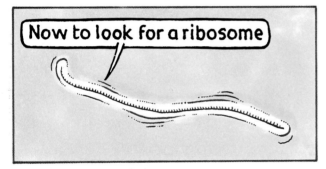

The copy strand finds a ribosome (which isn't too hard, because there are thousands in each cell).

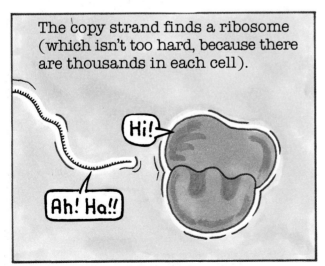

And all this happens millions of times each minute, every day, inside the cells of your body.

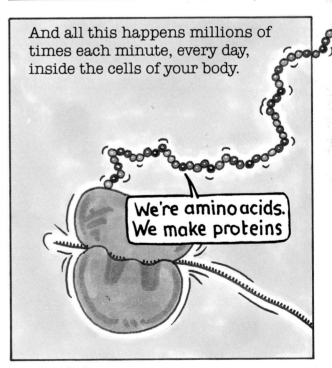

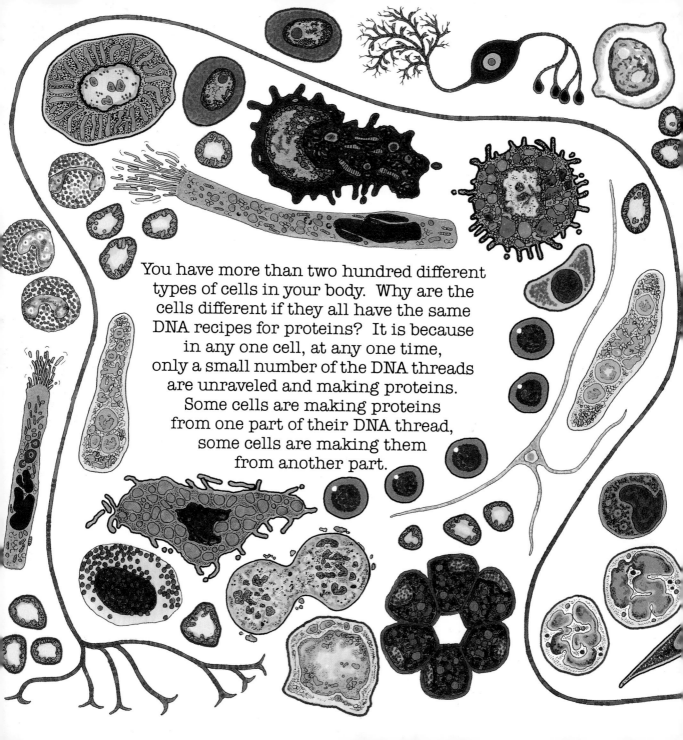

You have more than two hundred different
types of cells in your body. Why are the
cells different if they all have the same
DNA recipes for proteins? It is because
in any one cell, at any one time,
only a small number of the DNA threads
are unraveled and making proteins.
Some cells are making proteins
from one part of their DNA thread,
some cells are making them
from another part.

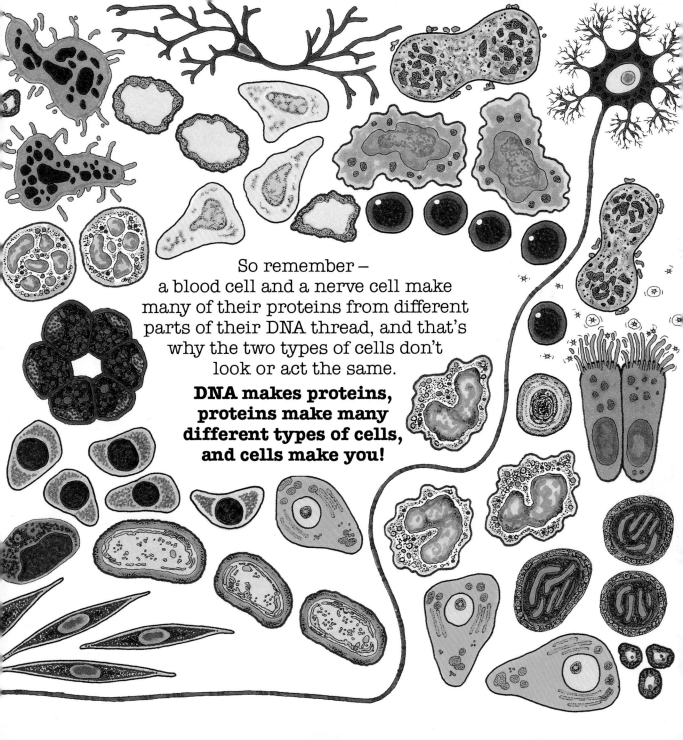

So remember –
a blood cell and a nerve cell make
many of their proteins from different
parts of their DNA thread, and that's
why the two types of cells don't
look or act the same.

**DNA makes proteins,
proteins make many
different types of cells,
and cells make you!**

Human beings come in all shapes, sizes, and colors, although
they are pretty much the same inside. Why do we all look
different? Because our DNA plans are all slightly different.

Human DNA is divided into genes, which are the recipes for
proteins. Many genes make the same proteins in all human
beings. In fact, about 99.5 percent of your DNA is in the same
order as everybody else's.

But some parts of our DNA plans vary. Your hair color genes may have recipes for blonde, brown, black, or red hair. Genes for eye color may make your eyes blue, brown, hazel, or green. Genes for skin color may make you different shades of pink, yellow, or brown. We are all slightly different from one another because of the proteins our cells make. Long before you were born, one tiny part of your DNA determined whether you were going to be a boy or a girl.

Some illnesses are caused by problems in the DNA plan. These problems mean that a protein is not made correctly or is not made at all. This means that some cells can't do their jobs properly. Diseases like muscular dystrophy and cystic fibrosis are caused by problems in DNA. Scientists all over the world are trying to unlock the secrets of our DNA plans in the biggest biology experiment ever. Computers are storing lists of the enormous amount of information in human DNA. Imagine how hard that is – your DNA threads contain six billion **A**s, **T**s, **C**s, and **G**s, three billion on each side of the double helix! Imagine that each of your 46 chromosomes is a large volume of an encyclopedia. On every page of each volume of this encyclopedia would be the recipes for making all the different proteins in your body, written down in millions of **A**s, **T**s, **C**s, and **G**s.

We've told you the story of
human DNA, but there are
millions of other life forms on this planet,
and millions more that are now extinct. Your body
is very different from that of a caterpillar or a crab,
a killer whale or a bat. And (we hope) you don't look anything
like a spider or a giant tree! Surely all these living things must
have different chemical plans inside them, right? Well, no – the
amazing fact is that everything that lives on earth has DNA
plans that are made of the same basic chemicals as yours. All
living things have DNA in a double helix made of **A**s, **T**s, **C**s,
and **G**s. So why don't all living things look and behave the
same way? Because each species of plant and animal has **A**s,
Ts, **C**s, and **G**s in a different order along its DNA. The DNA
makes different proteins, those proteins make different cells,
and those cells make different life forms. And these life forms
all evolved from the first single-celled creatures found millions
of years ago. Over millions of years, slight mistakes have been
made in copying DNA, and so different species have slowly
developed, each perfectly suited to its surroundings.

I suppose you realize
that if my DNA had been
in a different order,
I could have been a
brain surgeon!